ROYAL COURT

The Royal Court Theatre presents

The National Theatre of Scotland production of

THE STRANGE UNDOING OF PRUDENCIA HART

by David Greig

THE STRANGE UNDOING OF PRUDENCIA HART was conceived and devised by David Greig and Wils Wilson. It was first presented by the National Theatre of Scotland in the Victorian Bar of the Tron Theatre, Glasgow, on Thursday 10th February 2011. The original cast, in alphabetical order, was as follows:

Andy Clark
Annie Grace
Alasdair Macrae
David McKay
Madeline Worrall

The original creative team was as follows:

Director Wils Wilson
Designer Georgia McGuinness
Composer Alasdair Macrae
Movement Director Janice Parker
Casting Director Anne Henderson

THE STRANGE UNDOING OF PRUDENCIA HART was first performed in London at the London Welsh Centre, King's Cross, on Friday 12th July 2013 as part of the Royal Court's Theatre Local strand of site-specific work.

D1643267

KA 0377213 6

THE STRANGE UNDOING OF PRUDENCIA HART

by David Greig

Cast (in alphabetical order)
Annie Grace
Melody Grove
Alasdair Macrae
Paul McCole
David McKay

Director **Wils Wilson**
Designer **Georgia McGuinness**
Composer & Musical Director **Alasdair Macrae**
Movement Director **Janice Parker**
Casting Director **Anne Henderson**
Company Stage Manager **Gary Morgan**
Assistant Stage Manager **Thomas Chappell**

The Royal Court, The National Theatre of Scotland and Stage Management wish to thank the
following for their help with this production:
Rhian Jones, Karen Gregory and all at the London Welsh Centre, Mickey Smith, Saija Kamarainen,
Lucca Joy Barratt and all at the Bussey Building, Liz Smith, Emma Callander.

UNIVERSITY OF WINCHESTER
LIBRARY

THE COMPANY

DAVID GREIG (Writer)

THEATRE INCLUDES: Dalgety, Being Norwegian (Òran Mór/Theatre Uncut); Charlie & the Chocolate Factory (Theatre Royal, Drury Lane); One Day in Spring, Dunsinane, Peter Pan, The Bacchae, Gobbo (National Theatre of Scotland); Yellow Moon, The Monster in the Hall, Dr Korczak's Example, Petra (TAG); The Architect, Midsummer, Damascus, Outlying Islands (Traverse); The American Pilot (RSC); The Letter of Last Resort, Miniskirts of Kabul (Tricycle); Pyrenees (Paines Plough); The Cosmonaut's Last Message to the Woman He Once Loved in the Former Soviet Union (Paines Plough/ Tron); San Diego (Tron); Futurology, 8000M, Lament, Mainstream, Timeless, Airport (Suspect Culture).

ANNIE GRACE (Cast)

THEATRE INCLUDES: Peter Pan (National Theatre of Scotland); A Little Bit of Northern Light (Scottish Opera); Para Handy (Open Work); Thank God for John Muir, Cyrano De Bergerac, Tir na nOg, Poker Alice (Òran Mór); The Heretic's Tale, Jacobite Country (Dogstar); Tom O'Shanter (Perth Theatre); Pinocchio (Arches); Mum's the Word (Robert C. Kelly); The Celtic Story (Wildcat); Homers (Traverse); The Accidental Death of an Accordionist, The Wedding (Right Lines); Miniatures (Theatre Collective).

Annie was a founder member of the band Iron Horse with whom she toured worldwide for several years.

MELODY GROVE (Cast)

THEATRE INCLUDES: The Importance of Being Earnest (Lyric, Belfast/Royal Lyceum); Of Mice & Men (Royal Lyceum); 2401 Objects (Analogue/Pleasance); Snow White & the Seven De'Wharffs (Macrobert); Room, One Night Stand, One Thousand Paper Cranes (Tron); The Girls of Slender Means (Stellar Quines/Assembly Rooms).

FILM INCLUDES: The True Story of Bonnie Parker, A Stately Suicide, Venus & the Sun, Sisters.

RADIO INCLUDES: The Grapes of Wrath, The Great Gatsby, The Call of the Wild, The Voysey Inheritance, A Case for Paul Temple, The Vanishing, Of Mice & Men, La Princesse de Clèves, The Importance of Being Emma, The Child Inside.

AWARDS INCLUDE: The James Bridie Gold Medal for Acting (Royal Scottish Academy of Music & Drama).

ALASDAIR MACRAE (Cast, Composer & Musical Director)

THEATRE INCLUDES: Calum's Road, Tall Tales for Small People, Peter Pan, Peeping at Bosch, Gobbo, HOME Caithness (National Theatre of Scotland); The Undersea World of Bubble McBea (Scottish Opera); Fergus Lamont (Communicado); Lost Ones, Invisible Man (Vanishing Point); Homers (Traverse); Our Bad Magnet (Tron).

AS A MUSICAL DIRECTOR, SOUND DESIGNER & COMPOSER: Calum's Road, Tall Tales for Small People, Gobbo, HOME Caithness (National Theatre of Scotland); Anna Karenina, Sleeping Beauty (Dundee Rep); The Bookie (Cumbernauld); The Government Inspector (Communicado); Little Red Riding Hood (Arches); The Beggar's Opera (Vanishing Point/Royal Lyceum/Belgrade, Coventry/Tramway); Subway (Vanishing Point); Interiors (Vanishing Point/Traverse/Festival Teatro Napoli); Tam O'Shanter (Communicado/Perth Rep).

AWARDS INCLUDE: Critics' Award for Theatre in Scotland for Best Music & Sound (The Strange Undoing of Prudencia Hart); Herald Angel Award, Scotsman Fringe First & Critics' Award for Theatre in Scotland (Subway & Government Inspector); Newcastleton Traditional Music Festival Border Ballad

Competition (Second Place).

PAUL McCOLE (Cast)

THEATRE INCLUDES: Ski Sluts from Glenshee (Theatre Works); Beyond the Pale (Theatre Tribe); Blood Wedding, Romeo & Juliet (Citizens).

TELEVISION INCLUDES: Sunshine on Leith, Case Histories, Up There, Doors Open, Rab C Nesbitt, Jimmy's Show, Still Game, Dear Green Place, Crying With Laughter, Rebus, High Times, The Key, Taggart.

FILM INCLUDES: Blackout, Electric Blues, Killer, The Stain, Dignitas: The Movie.

GEORGIA McGUINNESS (Designer)

FOR THE ROYAL COURT: Crave (& Paines Plough).

THEATRE INCLUDES: The Miracle Man, Empty, 365 (National Theatre of Scotland); Midsummer, Perfect Days, Abandonment (Traverse); Arabian Nights (RSC); Curse of the Starving Class (Royal Lyceum); Yarn (Grid Iron/Dundee Rep); Helter Skelter (Tramway/Music at the Brewhouse); Green Whale (Licketyspit); Arabian Nights (Young Vic/International tour); The Cosmonaut's Last Message to the Woman He Once Loved in the Former Soviet Union, Sleeping Around, Crazy Gary's Mobile Disco (Paines Plough); Caravan (National Theatre of Norway); Afore Night Come (Clwyd); The Importance of Being Earnest (Nottingham Playhouse); The Weavers (Gate); Twelfth Night (Central School of Speech & Drama); The Sunset Ship (Young Vic/National Gallery); Othello (Watermill); King & Marshall (Bloomsbury); Four Saints in Three Acts (Trinity Opera).

DAVID McKAY (Cast)

THEATRE INCLUDES: A Satire of the Three Estates (Linlithgow Palace); Dreams & Other Nightmares (Tron), Aalst (National Theatre of Scotland); The Apprentice (Òran Mór); Four Men & a Poker Game (Metis); The Tempest, Salvation (Tron); Wishing Tree, Damaged Goods (Wiseguise); One, Two, Hey! (Traverse); The Conquest of the South Pole (Raindog); Of Mice & Men (Brunton, Musselburgh); Shining Souls, Hansel & Gretel, The Lion the Witch & the Wardrobe (Citizens); As You Like It, The Game's a Bogie (Scottish tour); Ten Days in May, Pals (Cumbernauld); Smugglers, Tellyitis (Borderline); The Celtic Story, Harmony Row (Wildcat); The Big Move (Skint Knees); Wuthering Heights (Birds of Paradise); Hair of the Dog (Dependency Culture).

TELEVISION INCLUDES: Shoe Box Zoo, Hamish Macbeth, Looking After Jo-Jo, The Tales of Para Handy, Down Among the Big Boys, Justice Games, Down Where the Buffalo Go, Workhorses, Rab C Nesbitt, Rookie, Taggart.

FILM INCLUDES: Village on the Roof, The Gift, Neds, Ae Fond Kiss, Once Upon a Time in the Midlands, My Name is Joe, Les Miserable, Braveheart, Initiation, Close, Nightlife, Joyride, The Girl in the Picture, As Far As You've Come.

JANICE PARKER (Movement Director)

THEATRE INCLUDES: Private Party (Janice Parker Projects/ The Arches); The Albert Drive Project Glas(s) Performance/ Tramway); Ignition, Ménage à Trois, Truant (National Theatre of Scotland); Kes (Catherine Wheels); Age of Arousal (Stellar Quines/Royal Lyceum, Edinburgh); The Girls of Slender Means (Stella Quines/Assembly); The Killing Times, The Love Adventures of Geordie Cochrane, Willie Nastle (Rowan Tree); Exotic Hyper Space, Instant Travel to Pop Up Cities (Lung Ha's).

AWARDS INCLUDE: Herald Angel Award, Unlimited Cutural Olympiad Commission (Private Dancer); Janice is a Creative Scotland Award recipient.

WILS WILSON (Director)

THEATRE INCLUDES: Praxis Makes Perfect (National Theatre Wales); Ignition, Gobbo, HOME Shetland (National Theatre of Scotland); HOUSE, Mapping the Edge, News from the Seventh Floor, Mulgrave (wilson+wilson); Manchester Lines (Library Theatre Company, Manchester); Secret Heart, Eliza's House (Royal Exchange, Manchester).

AWARDS INCLUDE: Critics' Awards for Theatre in Scotland for Best Production for Children & Young People (Gobbo); Critics' Awards for Theatre in Scotland for Best Music (HOME Shetland, The Strange Undoing of Prudencia Hart); Herald Angel Award ((The Strange Undoing of Prudencia Hart).

Wils was co-founder and co-Artistic Director of wilson+wilson (1997-2007), creating site-specific installation and theatre.

ABOUT
THE NATIONAL THEATRE OF SCOTLAND

[**NATIONAL THEATRE OF SCOTLAND**]

It is our ambition to make incredible theatre experiences for you, which will stay in your heart and mind long after you have gone home.

We tirelessly seek the stories which need to be told and retold, the voices which need to be heard and the sparks that need to be ignited. We do this with an ever-evolving community of play-makers, maverick thinkers and theatre crusaders. We try to be technically adventurous and fearlessly collaborative. We are what our artists, performers and participants make us. And with no stage of our own, we have the freedom to go where our audiences and stories take us. There is no limit to what we believe theatre can be, no limit to the stories we are able to tell, no limit to the possibilities of our imaginations.

All of Scotland is our stage, and from here we perform to the world. We are a theatre of the imagination: a Theatre Without Walls.

For the latest information on all our activities, visit our online home at www.nationaltheatrescotland.com

Follow us on Twitter @NTSonline and join in the conversation #PrudenciaHart

Find us on Facebook: NationalTheatreScotland

 All information correct at time of going to press and subject to change. The National Theatre of Scotland reserves the right to alter casts, performances, seating or ticket arrangements and latecomers may not be admitted. Booking fees may apply on tickets, please check with the venue Box Office when booking. The National Theatre of Scotland, a company limited by guarantee and registered in Scotland (SC234270), is a registered Scottish charity (SCO33377). The National Theatre of Scotland is core funded by the Scottish Government.

BENROMACH SPEYSIDE SINGLE MALT SCOTCH WHISKY

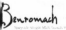

Benromach Speyside Single Malt Scotch Whisky is proud to work with the National Theatre of Scotland and support this performance of The Strange Undoing of Prudencia Hart.

www.benromach.com

facebook.com/Benromach

twitter.com/Benromach

drinkaware.co.uk
for the facts about alcohol

THE ENGLISH STAGE COMPANY AT THE ROYAL COURT THEATRE

'For me the theatre is really a religion or way of life. You must decide what you feel the world is about and what you want to say about it, so that everything in the theatre you work in is saying the same thing ... A theatre must have a recognisable attitude. It will have one, whether you like it or not.'

George Devine, first artistic director of the English Stage Company: notes for an unwritten book.

photo: Stephen Cummiskey

As Britain's leading national company dedicated to new work, the Royal Court Theatre produces new plays of the highest quality, working with writers from all backgrounds, and addressing the problems and possibilities of our time.

"The Royal Court has been at the centre of British cultural life for the past 50 years, an engine room for new writing and constantly transforming the theatrical culture." Stephen Daldry

Since its foundation in 1956, the Royal Court has presented premieres by almost every leading contemporary British playwright, from John Osborne's Look Back in Anger to Caryl Churchill's A Number and Tom Stoppard's Rock 'n' Roll. Just some of the other writers to have chosen the Royal Court to premiere their work include Edward Albee, John Arden, Richard Bean, Samuel Beckett, Edward Bond, Leo Butler, Jez Butterworth, Martin Crimp, Ariel Dorfman, Stella Feehily, Christopher Hampton, David Hare, Eugène Ionesco, Ann Jellicoe, Terry Johnson, Sarah Kane, David Mamet, Martin McDonagh, Conor McPherson, Joe Penhall, Lucy Prebble, Mark Ravenhill, Simon Stephens, Wole Soyinka, Polly Stenham, David Storey, Debbie Tucker Green, Arnold Wesker and Roy Williams.

"It is risky to miss a production there." Financial Times

In addition to its full-scale productions, the Royal Court also facilitates international work at a grass roots level, developing exchanges which bring young writers to Britain and sending British writers, actors and directors to work with artists around the world. The research and play development arm of the Royal Court Theatre, The Studio, finds the most exciting and diverse range of new voices in the UK. The Studio runs play-writing groups including the Young Writers Programme, Critical Mass for black, Asian and minority ethnic writers and the biennial Young Writers Festival. For further information, go to www.royalcourttheatre.com/playwriting/the-studio.

ROYAL COURT SUPPORTERS

The Royal Court has significant and longstanding relationships with many organisations and individuals who provide vital support. It is this support that makes possible its unique playwriting and audience development programmes.

Open Court & Theatre Local are supported by Bloomberg. The Genesis Foundation supports the Royal Court's work with International Playwrights. The Jerwood Charitable Foundation supports emerging writers through the Jerwood New Playwrights programme. The Andrew Lloyd Webber Foundation supports the Royal Court's Studio, which aims to seek out, nurture and support emerging playwrights.

The Harold Pinter Playwright's Award is given annually by his widow, Lady Antonia Fraser, to support a new commission at the Royal Court.

PUBLIC FUNDING
Arts Council England, London
British Council
European Commission Representation in the UK

CHARITABLE DONATIONS
Martin Bowley Charitable Trust
Columbia Foundation Fund of the London
Community Foundation
Cowley Charitable Trust
The Dorset Foundation
The John Ellerman Foundation
The Eranda Foundation
Genesis Foundation
J Paul Getty Jnr Charitable Trust
The Golden Bottle Trust
The Haberdashers' Company
Jerwood Charitable Foundation
Marina Kleinwort Trust
The Andrew Lloyd Webber Foundation
John Lyon's Charity
The Andrew W. Mellon Foundation
Rose Foundation
The Royal College of Psychiatrists
Royal Victoria Hall Foundation
The Dr Mortimer & Theresa Sackler Foundation
John Thaw Foundation
The Vandervell Foundation
The Garfield Weston Foundation

Theatre Local and Open Court supported by

Bloomberg

Supported by
ARTS COUNCIL
ENGLAND

CORPORATE SUPPORTERS & SPONSORS
American Airlines
BBC
Bloomberg
Café Colbert
Cream
Coutts
Ecosse Films
Kudos Film & Television
MAC
Moët & Chandon
Oakley Capital Limited
Smythson of Bond Street
White Light Ltd

BUSINESS ASSOCIATES, MEMBERS & BENEFACTORS
Annoushka
Auerbach & Steele Opticians
Bank of America Merrill Lynch
Byfield Consultancy
Hugo Boss
Lazard
Savills
Troy Asset Management
Vanity Fair
Waterman Group

DEVELOPMENT ADVOCATES
John Ayton MBE
Elizabeth Bandeen
Kinvara Balfour
Anthony Burton CBE
Piers Butler
Sindy Caplan
Sarah Chappatte
Cas Donald (Vice Chair)
Celeste Fenichel
Emma Marsh (Chair)
Deborah Shaw Marquardt (Vice Chair)
Tom Siebens
Sian Westerman
Daniel Winterfeldt

INDIVIDUAL MEMBERS

MAJOR DONORS
Eric Abraham
Rob & Siri Cope
Cas Donald
Richard & Marcia Grand
Jack & Linda Keenan
Adam Kenwright
Miles Morland
NoraLee & Jon Sedmak
Deborah Shaw & Stephen Marquardt
Jan & Michael Topham
Monica B Voldstad

MOVER-SHAKERS
Anonymous
Christine Collins
Jordan Cook
Piers & Melanie Gibson
Lydia & Manfred Gorvy
Mr & Mrs Roderick Jack
Duncan Matthews QC
Ian & Carol Sellars

BOUNDARY-BREAKERS
Anonymous
Katie Bradford
David Harding
Madeleine Hodgkin
Philip & Joan Kingsley
Emma Marsh
Philippa Thorp
Edgar & Judith Wallner
Mr & Mrs Nick Wheeler

GROUND-BREAKERS
Anonymous
Allen Appen & Jane Wiest
Moira Andreae
Mr & Mrs Simon Andrews
Nick Archdale
Charlotte Asprey
Jane Attias
Brian Balfour-Oatts
Elizabeth & Adam Bandeen
Ray Barrell & Ursula Van Almsick
Dr Kate Best

Sarah & David Blomfield
Stan & Val Bond
Kristina Borsy & Nick Turdean
Neil & Sarah Brener
Deborah Brett
Joanna Buckenham
Lois Moore & Nigel Burridge
Louise Burton
Helena Butler
Piers Butler
Sindy & Jonathan Caplan
Gavin & Lesley Casey
Sarah & Philippe Chappatte
Tim & Caroline Clark
Carole & Neville Conrad
Andrea & Anthony Coombs
Clyde Cooper
Ian & Caroline Cormack
Mr & Mrs Cross
Andrew & Amanda Cryer
Alison Davies
Roger & Alison De Haan
Noel De Keyzer
Matthew Dean
Polly Devlin OBE
Sophie Diedrichs-Cox
Denise & Randolph Dumas
Robyn Durie
Glenn & Phyllida Earle
The Edwin Fox Foundation
Lisa Erikson & Edward Ocampo
Mark & Sarah Evans
Celeste & Peter Fenichel
Deborah Ferreira
Beverley Gee
Nick & Julie Gould
Lord & Lady Grabiner
Reade & Elizabeth Griffith
Sue & Don Guiney
Jill Hackel & Andrzej Zarzycki
Carol Hall

Jennifer & Stephen Harper
Mr & Mrs Sam Haubold
Mr & Mrs Gordon Holmes
Damien Hyland
Suzie & David Hyman
Amanda Ibbetson
Nicholas Jones
David P Kaskel & Christopher A Teano
Vincent & Amanda Keaveny
Peter & Maria Kellner
Nicola Kerr
Steve Kingshott
Mr & Mrs Pawel Kisielewski
David & Sarah Kowitz
Rosemary Leith
Larry & Peggy Levy
Imelda Liddiard
Daisy & Richard Littler
Kathryn Ludlow
Beatrice & James Lupton CBE
Dr Ekaterina Malievskaia & George Goldsmith
Christopher Marek Rencki
Mrs Janet Martin
Andrew McIver
Barbara Minto
Angelie Moledina
Ann & Gavin Neath CBE
Clive & Annie Norton
Georgia Oetker
James Orme-Smith
Mr & Mrs Sandy Orr
Mr & Mrs Guy Paterson
Sir William & Lady Vanessa Patey
William Plapinger & Cassie Murray
Andrea & Hilary Ponti
Lauren Prakke
Annie & Preben Prebensen
Wendy & Philip Press
Mrs Ivetta Rabinovich
Julie Ritter
Mark & Tricia Robinson
Paul & Gill Robinson
Corinne Rooney
Sir & Lady Ruddock
William & Hilary Russell

Julie & Bill Ryan
Sally & Anthony Salz
Bhags Sharma
J Sheridan
The Michael & Melanie Sherwood Charitable Foundation
Tom Siebens & Mimi Parsons
Andy Simpkin
Anthony Simpson & Susan Boster
Andrea Sinclair &
Serge Kremer
Paul & Rita Skinner
Mr & Mrs RAH Smart
Brian Smith
Barbara Soper
Zeina & Saadi Soudavar
Sue St Johns
The Ulrich Family
The Ury Trust
Amanda Vail
Constanze Von Unruh
Ian & Victoria Watson & The Watson Foundation
Matthew & Sian Westerman
Anne-Marie Williams
Sir Robert & Lady Wilson
Mr Daniel Winterfeldt & Mr Jonathan Leonhart
Martin & Sally Woodcock
Katherine & Michael Yates

With thanks to our Friends, Stage-Taker and Ice-Breaker members whose support we greatly appreciate.

FOR THE ROYAL COURT

Royal Court Theatre, Sloane Square, London SW1W 8AS
Tel: 020 7565 5050 Fax: 020 7565 5001
info@royalcourttheatre.com, www.royalcourttheatre.com

Artistic Director **Vicky Featherstone**
Associate Directors **Carrie Cracknell, Simon Godwin, John Tiffany**
Artistic Associate **Emily McLaughlin***
Diversity Associate **Ola Animashawun***
Education Associate **Lynne Gagliano***
PA to the Artistic & Executive Director **Sarah Hopkins**
Trainee Director **Ned Bennett ‡**

Literary Manager **Christopher Campbell**
Senior Reader **Carissa Hope Lynch***
Literary Assistant **Louise Stephens Alexander**
Studio Administrator **Chloe Todd Fordham***
Writers' Tutor **Leo Butler***

Associate Director International **Elyse Dodgson**
International Projects Manager **Chris James**
International Associate **Richard Twyman**

Casting Director **Amy Ball**
Casting Assistant **Lotte Hines**

Head of Production **Niall Black**
Production Manager **Tariq Rifaat**
Production Assistant **Zoe Hurwitz**
Head of Lighting **Jack Williams**
Lighting Deputy **Marec Joyce**
Lighting Assistants **Jess Faulks & Sam Smallman**
Lighting Board Operator **Laura Whitley**
Head of Stage **Steven Stickler**
Stage Deputy **Dan Lockett**
Stage Chargehand **Lee Crimmen**
Chargehand & Building Maintenance Technician **Matt Livesey**
Head of Sound **David McSeveney**
Sound Deputy **Emily Legg**
Sound Operator **Joel Price**

Head of Costume **Iona Kenrick**
Costume Deputy **Jackie Orton**
Wardrobe Assistant **Pam Anson**

ENGLISH STAGE COMPANY

President
Dame Joan Plowright CBE

Honorary Council
Sir Richard Eyre CBE
Alan Grieve CBE
Martin Paisner CBE

Council
Chairman **Anthony Burton CBE**
Vice Chairman **Graham Devlin CBE**

Executive Producer **Lucy Davies**
General Manager **Catherine Thornborrow**
Administrator **Holly Gladwell**
Associate Producer **Daniel Brodie**

Finance Director **Helen Perryer**
Finance Manager **Martin Wheeler**
Finance Officer **Rachel Harrison***
Finance & Administration Assistant **Rosie Mortimer**

Head of Marketing & Sales **Becky Wootton**
Marketing Manager (Maternity Leave) **Ruth Waters**
Marketing Manager (Maternity Cover) **Sebastian Stern**
Press & Public Relations Officer **Anna Evans**
Communications Officer **Dion Wilson**
Communications Assistant **Rachel Pronger** & **Phoebe Eclair-Powell**

Sales Manager **Liam Geoghegan**
Deputy Sales Manager **Áine O'Sullivan**
Box Office Sales Assistants **Ryan Govin, Joe Hodgson, Chelsea Nelson, Zainab Hassan*, Helen Preddy*, Rachel Pronger*.**

Head of Development **Rebecca Smith**
Senior Development Manager **Sue Livermore**
Development Managers **Lucy Buxton, Luciana Lawlor, Anna Sampson**
Development Assistant **Kate Garbutt**

Theatre Manager **Bobbie Stokes**
Front of House Manager **Rachel Dudley**
Theatre Assistant **Chris Sonnex**
Events Manager **Joanna Ostrom***
Duty Managers **Michael Bond*, Elinor Keber*, Helen Matravers*, Mila Rosser*, Tanya Shields***
Bar & Food Manager **Sami Rifaat**
Deputy Bar & Food Manager (Interim Cover) **Siobhan Lightfoot**
Bar and Food Supervisor **Jared Thomas**
Head Chef **Tim Jenner**
Sous Chef **Paulino Chuitcheu**
Bookshop Manager **Simon David**
Bookshop Assistant **Vanessa Hammick***
Stage Door/Reception **Paul Lovegrove, Tyrone Lucas**

Thanks to all of our ushers and bar staff.

‡ The post of Trainee Director is supported by an anonymous donor.

This theatre has the support of the Pearson Playwrights' Scheme sponsored by the Peggy Ramsay Foundation.

* Part-time.

Members
Jennette Arnold OBE
Judy Daish
Sir David Green KCMG
Joyce Hytner OBE
Stephen Jeffreys
Wasfi Kani OBE
Phyllida Lloyd CBE
James Midgley
Sophie Okonedo OBE
Alan Rickman
Anita Scott
Katharine Viner
Lord Stewart Wood

The Strange Undoing of Prudencia Hart

David Greig was born in Edinburgh. His plays include *Europe*, *The Architect*, *The Speculator*, *The Cosmonaut's Last Message to the Woman He Once Loved in the Former Soviet Union*, *Outlying Islands*, *San Diego*, *Pyrenees*, *The American Pilot*, *Yellow Moon: The Ballad of Leila and Lee*, *Damascus*, *Midsummer* (*a Play with Songs*) and *Dunsinane*. In 1990 he co-founded Suspect Culture to produce collaborative, experimental theatre work. His translations and adaptations include Camus's *Caligula*, Euripides' *The Bacchae*, Strindberg's *Creditors* and *Peter Pan*.

by the same author

OUTLYING ISLANDS
SAN DIEGO
PYRENEES
THE AMERICAN PILOT
YELLOW MOON
DAMASCUS
MIDSUMMER (A PLAY WITH SONGS)
DUNSINANE

SELECTED PLAYS 1999–2009
*(San Diego, Outlying Islands, Pyrenees, The American Pilot,
Being Norwegian, Kyoto, Brewers Fayre)*

adaptations
CAMUS'S CALIGULA
EURIPIDES' THE BACCHAE
AUGUST STRINDBERG'S CREDITORS

with Suspect Culture
CASANOVA

Published by Methuen

DAVID GREIG PLAYS: I
*(Europe, The Architect, The Cosmonaut's Last Message
to the Woman He Once Loved in the Former Soviet Union)*

VICTORIA

DAVID GREIG

The Strange Undoing of
Prudencia Hart

faber and faber

First published in 2011
by Faber and Faber Limited
74–77 Great Russell Street, London WC1B 3DA

Typeset by Country Setting, Kingsdown, Kent CT14 8ES
Printed in England by CPI Group (UK) Ltd, Croydon, CR0 4YY

All rights reserved

Copyright © David Greig, 2011

David Greig is hereby identified as author of
this work in accordance with Section 77 of the
Copyright, Designs and Patents Act 1988

All rights whatsoever in this work, amateur or professional,
are strictly reserved. Applications for permission for any use
whatsoever, including performance rights, must be made in advance,
prior to any such proposed use, to Casarotto Ramsay & Associates Ltd,
Waverley House, 7–12 Noel Street, London W1F 8GQ

No performance may be given unless a licence
has first been obtained

*This book is sold subject to the condition that it shall not, by
way of trade or otherwise, be lent, resold, hired out or otherwise
circulated without the publisher's prior consent in any form of
binding or cover other than that in which it is published and
without a similar condition including this condition being
imposed on the subsequent purchaser*

A CIP record for this book
is available from the British Library

ISBN 978-0-571-30998-6

2 4 6 8 10 9 7 5 3

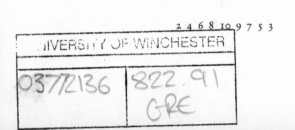
UNIVERSITY OF WINCHESTER

03772136   822.91
GRE

Author's Note

Sometime in the summer of 2006 Wils Wilson and I came up with the idea of a theatre ballad to be told in a pub. I'm pretty sure we were sitting round a camp fire but that might just be my mind making a story out of it. As we drank whisky and our teeth chattered through a chilly Scottish summer dimming, Wils and I imagined actors taking over a pub, telling a supernatural story, clambering over the bar and pub tables, playing the fiddle, singing, and drawing the audience into the world of a magical lock-in. We took the idea to Vicky Featherstone at the National Theatre of Scotland, who was immediately enthusiastic and who encouraged us to think about *The Border Ballads*.

Eventually, a small team of us went to Kelso for a weekend of research into *The Border Ballads*. During those two days we spoke to many people including the amazing Walter Elliot, who gave us the benefit of his vast knowledge of the folklore and people of the Borders. We were guests of the Kelso Folk Club (so unfairly traduced in the text here!). Aly played us ballads and supernatural songs and we met folk studies expert Valentina Bold who introduced us to a world of thought, ideas and passion for borders and for ballads of all kinds. That weekend we began to see the dim outlines of a story.

The story had to sit for a few more years before it could finally become a play. In December 2010, Wils, Georgia McGuinness and I gathered for a week's work in Scotland. On the day Wils arrived, almost the moment she set foot off the train, it began to snow. It snowed like it hadn't snowed in Scotland for thirty years. It snowed and it didn't stop. There were skiers in central Edinburgh and avalanche warnings on Arthur's Seat. We had to abandon our Highland retreat and instead hole up in my small village in Fife. There were no actors, no musicians and nothing else to do but while away the long cold winter nights by telling the events of Prudencia, again and again, back and forth to each other until finally, somehow, even without us noticing, it became a story: a story that felt like it had always been there. That was when I was finally able to write the ballad.

I would like to thank all the people who helped me shape the text of Prudencia, in particular the wonderful actors of the first company: Georgia McGuinness and Aly Macrae; Vicky Featherstone and the production team at the National Theatre of Scotland; Valentina Bold, who lent us the sparkle in her eyes; and of course, I would like to thank Wils Wilson for guiding the whole project with such imagination, patience and care.

The Strange Undoing of Prudencia Hart was conceived and devised by David Greig and Wils Wilson. It was first presented by the National Theatre of Scotland in the Victorian Bar of the Tron Theatre, Glasgow, on 10 February 2011. The cast, in alphabetical order, was as follows:

Andy Clark
Annie Grace
Alasdair Macrae
David McKay
Madeleine Worrall

Director Wils Wilson
Designer Georgia McGuinness
Musical Director Alasdair Macrae
Movement Director Janice Parker
Casting Director Anne Henderson

THE STRANGE UNDOING
OF PRUDENCIA HART

For Lucie

'Till a' the seas gang dry, my dear,
   And rocks melt wi' the sun
I will love thee still, my dear,
   Till a' the seas gang dry.'

Robert Burns

ONE

We're in a pub or a bar, a ceilidh place, a community hall, anywhere that people are gathered and warm and have enough drink.

A session is in progress.

A small band play a folk tune. The playing is rough and ready. There's room for players to join and leave the playing.

When the audience are settled the story begins.

Part the First

TWO

SONG: THE TWA CORBIES

As I was walking all alane,
I heard twa corbies makin a mane.
The tane unto the ither say,
'Whar sall we gang and dine the-day?'

'In ahint yon auld fail dyke,
I wot there lies a new slain knight;
And nane do ken that he lies there,
But his hawk, his hound an his lady fair.'

'His hound is tae the huntin gane,
His hawk tae fetch the wildfowl hame,
His lady's tain anither mate,
So we may mak oor dinner swate.'

'Ye'll sit on his white hause-bane,
And I'll pike oot his bonny blue een.
Wi ae lock o his gowden hair
We'll theek oor nest whan it grows bare.'

'Mony a one for him makes mane,
But nane sall ken whar he is gane;
Oer his white banes, whan they are bare,
The wind sall blaw for evermair.'

THREE

It's difficult to know where to start
With the strange undoing of Prudencia Hart.
Beginnings – as she herself often says –
Find characters *in medias res* –

So this undoing story could begin at the moment
Prudence realises the trouble she's in
Or the moment with the burning water,
Or the moment when the Devil caught her
Or the moment when the clocks all stopped
Or the moment when the midwife dropped
The babe Prudencia into the arms of a mother
Who obviously preferred her older brother
And so she became the pet of a father
Who faced with messy life would rather
Photograph every football ground in Fife,
Or alphabetise
All paperbacks of a certain size
And so Pru's and her dad's idea of a fun day
Was to browse away an endless Sunday
In second-hand bookshops making lists,
Of nineteenth-century German philatelists
Or – on one occasion a journey of two whole days –
To photograph the guitar that played Purple Haze –
It came in a case complete with plectrum –
Nowadays we'd say Mr Hart was autistic spectrum
But back then he was just odd.
And – whatever he was – whatever his spectra –
Prudencia's complex was Electra.
She loved her dad and he did protect her
Which explains why she became – ultimately – herself
   a collector.
A collector of folk music – song in particular –
Ballads in fact. Her matricular
Thesis was on Walter Scott's *Minstrelsy of the Scottish
   Border*
But we digress – let's keep things in order –
We won't begin with Prudencia's birth,
Or her use of objects to maintain self-worth,
Or the moment of her fatal wooing
Or even the moment of her undoing.

– NO.

In storytelling – that most misused of all arts –
Horses absolutely must not go ahead of carts.
A ballad starts where a ballad starts and
This is the start of Prudencia Hart's.

– Snow!

Snow falls.

Midwinter, 21st of December.

And all across Scotland there's a great white falling
down of the sky.

– A burial.

– Did you ever see snow like it?

– Not for years.

– Not for years and years and years.

Not since children wore caps and tacketty boots.

It was as if history had gone into reverse and the past
returned like a tide over a beach wiping out our
footprints so that all the mess and ugliness of modern
life was smoothed away and the world was once more
full of old pure things like sledges and rosy cheeks and
a genuine need for warming soups

Thought Prudencia Hart

Tides and blankness

As she drove south through a great bleezing blinding
blowing blizzard

South into the Borders.

This is exactly the sort of snow that if it were in a border
ballad would poetically presage some kind of doom for

an innocent heroine or an encounter on the moor with a
sprite or villain or the losing of the heroine's selfhood in
the great white emptiness of the night

She thought.

But this is not a ballad

She thought.

And so this is just snow.

And she smiled

All around her drivers pulled on to the hard shoulder
Ambient temperatures were getting colder
Travellers made for somewhere warm
So why did Prudencia smile at the storm?

Prudencia looked at the rest of the world as though it
    was quite absurd
She was above the common herd
These idiots unprepared, careless, unprotected
Unready of forecast, uncollected
Of thought – not like Prudencia.

Prudencia smiled.

She had put snow tyres on her Ka.

Prudencia Hart – then – was a prudent
Twenty-eight-year-old postgraduate student.
Her PhD was on the topography of Hell so
When she was asked to go to Kelso –
To contribute a paper and join the plenary
At a conference celebrating the sixteenth centenary
Of the founding of the linguistics chair
At the tiny university there –
A conference which was provisionally entitled –
And this annoyed her – remember that, it's vital

On the linguistics and transmission of oral narratives

And balladry open brackets (border ballads, neither
   border nor ballad question mark, close brackets)

She went.

Despite her titular misgivings
Every girl must make her living
And here was an important chance to tell
Her colleagues her new theory of Hell's
Inherent interiority in folk discourses
And she supposed, a lunch with at least three courses.
And probably there would also be
The chance to network and perhaps to see
If a publisher might take her work on the border ballads.
She wondered if the lunch would have
Cold meats, smorgasbord or salads?
She hated doing lectures while feeling bloated
She did it once – and – carelessly misquoted
Hogg – the Famous Ettrick Shepherd – he
Wasn't her subject but the mistake put in jeopardy
Her reputation for accuracy so now – when it came
   to the crunch -
She would never do presentations after lunch.
She glanced at the programme to see what time
Her talk was on and saw her colleague Dr Colin Syme
Was booked to talk on the plenary too.
If the thought of salads had briefly buoyed her
The thought of Colin just annoyed her.
Dr Colin Syme – blokeish, obsessed with his kit,
He'd eat himself if he was a biscuit –
Who – can you believe this – gets actual grants
For the recording and analysis of football chants.
And, as if there wasn't enough not to like
Colin Syme loved his effing motorbike.
Prudence looked out at the gathering snow
And wondered if perhaps he wouldn't go.
It couldn't be easy to ride in a blizzard

Even for him – the leather-clad lizard.
But even as she thought it – 'Shite!'
She glanced out her window to the right
And there he was – Colin Syme
Actually making quite decent time
As he passed her at a dangerous speed
Just after the signpost to Berwick on Tweed.
She gave a shiver of cold anticipation
As she imagined greeting him at registration.

— Hello Colin.

Hello Pru.

— How are you?

Fine. I saw your piece.

— Did you?

The one about Tam Lin.

— Oh that one.

What was it in?

— *Journal of Ballad Studies*, volume twenty-eight.

That's it – I thought it was . . . great.

— Great?

Sweet.

— Sweet!?

That's right.

— What's sweet about it?

Your naive nostalgia, didn't you see my tweet about it?

— No.

I love the way you cling to old forms. Pru –

The narrative ballad form – like an old shoe –
So comforting so very
Middle class and reactionary
Like quilting or crochet it's heritage art
And yet here we are at the start
Of the twenty-first century – please.
Folk moves on and so should folk studies
Working-class performativity
Isn't plainsong or ballad, it's all celebrity
It's *X Factor* – it's flash mobs – it's being on YouTube –
    oh
It's less Tam Lin and more like Su Bo.
I say it each time I see you Pru
But each time I see you it feels new
So we're here again and I'll say it again
Prudencia – you are, essentially, a librarian
Peddling a kind of romantic tosh.
Your time has passed Pru – bish bash bosh!

No – her day in Kelso did not thrill her
But her day in Kelso wouldn't kill her.
And even if dull Colin wronged her
What doesn't kill you makes you stronger.

FOUR

*The conference. The chairman bangs a gavel and brings
the plenary to order.*

Ladies and gentlemen welcome back
I hope you have enjoyed the lunchtime craic
Don't they say at academic beanos
The best talk happens over the cappuccinos?
But – no – forgive me – colleagues – I jest
As experts in Scottish folk studies go – this lot are the best
We've got a fantastic debate ahead of us.

'Border Ballads neither Border nor Ballad?' Discuss.

A pretty formidable panel was gathered on the small stage
A kind of human contents page
Of folk and ballad studies.
As well as Colin and Prudencia there was
Professor Macintosh from the University of Aberdeen
Whose negative reading technique had seen
'The Border Widow's Lament' explained as neither
A ballad nor about a widow nor a lament either.
In fact, he thought, it ought to be read
As a celebration of marriage instead
And, Professor Macintosh said he felt,
It was probably set in the central belt.

Last, occupying the token Gaelic berth
Was Siolaigha Smith, an MA Student from Perth
Siolaigha, spelt S–I–O–L–A–G–H–A.
Made a little theory go a very long way.
Death of the author stuff – you get the gist.
She called hereself a post-post-structuralist,
Irritating Pru – an old-fashioned girl who preferred
Meaning still firmly attached to word.
But still she smiled as Siolaigh
Paraded the stuff she'd come to say.

'Borders and ballads both are discourses
Obsessed with separating opposing forces
That which is one and that which is the other
Father–son – England–Scotland – daughter–mother
So that if we look for example at the battle
Narratives of the rievers stealing cattle
Poems where 'us' resists a numerically
Larger 'them', we see maleness hysterically
Corral the female 'cow' or 'herd'
Not unlike the male poet corralling the female 'word'
And can it be coincidence that the 'Borders' or 'debatable
   lands'

18

Are always described as being in control of male hands?
But – in geography as in art – there is always a line
Almost impossible to define
A space where possibility hides
A female space in between the sides
These – indefinite-definition-givers –
In geography are almost always rivers
So is it possible to say –
If I may?
That ballads come not from the Borders – no indeed,
But they are born from the Vaginal Tweed.'

'Sioliagha,' thought Prudencia wearily
As they clapped the genital reference cheerily
That Celtic name which so endeared her
Was just a poncy way of spelling Sheila.

Next Colin spoke.

As usual he began with a joke.

About being a bloke.

'Last time I was here
I drank an awful lot of beer.'

   Laughter.

As he rattled through his usual patter –
Pru noticed he was getting fatter –
His talk drew out the patterns giving
Modern living
Narratives of a ballad-like fit –
To wit
The way stories from reality TV
And singers of karaoke
And street landscapes as described by rappers
And the battle narratives of happy slappers
Were all examples of folkloric invention
Every bit as deserving of our attention

As those collected by Sir Walter Scott
Who collected ballads – did he not? –
As a political act. Everybody knows his plan
Was to respond to the eighteenth-century popularity
    of *Ossian*
By collecting Scots poems, laments and sagas
To create a 'Scottish' identity 'every bit as artificial as
    Lady Gaga's'.

Putting 'Scottish' in air quote
Made Prudencia want to punch him in the throat
And as he said 'Gaga' he bowed with *faux* deference
As if to underline his pop-culture reference.

And so on and on and on Colin went
And Prudencia saw that he was bent
On producing a parade of ugliness as if all the art
And the feeling of the human heart
And songs, and stories and all the great
Examples of the BASIC HUMAN URGE TO CREATE

Were of no more importance than
A schoolgirl's Facebook status update.

Prudencia felt depressed.
Maybe she should go home, maybe that would be best.

She sat on the extreme left of the group – just there –
And the stage was small which meant her chair
Was just teetering on the edge of the stage
And Prudencia was struggling to engage
Her brain, it was after lunch and she was feeling bloated
And she hated the ideas that were being floated
The points that everyone was missing
And the intellectual wind into which she was so obviously
    pissing.

And Siolaigha or was it Shelia or Celia or Celery
Was giggling at everything Colin said so unbelievably
    predictably.

Ms Hart – Ms Hart?

— Mmm?!

Ms Hart – I expect you're ready to give
Us all a more traditional perspective –
In the light of what we're speaking about today
Can I ask Ms Hart – or Prudencia – if I may?
What exactly is the 'topography of Hell' anyway?

Prudencia rises to speak.

— Well
The topography of Hell is sort of like the geography
   of Hell
But it's more about the way that folk and folk songs tell
Stories about the Devil and his supernatural habitat
The images, the erotic tropes, the landscape and the
   details that
Make up Hell: and by asking 'what is Hell like?' – if you
   like – we
Can explore Hell's place in the collective psyche.
In particular we can look at the supernatural visits
Fair maidens make to the underworld – and ask if it's
Interesting the way the Devil is represented,
Sometimes as sane, sometimes demented
Sometimes male, sometimes female, like in
The supernatural ballad 'Tam Lin'.

But even as Pru spoke she saw the audience drift away
And she heard a yawn from Siolaigh
And who heated this room anyway?
And she felt the conference fade away.
As outside the snow fell and her head
Drooped as she dreamed of a cool bed
Of Egyptian cotton sheets, of snow
All crisp and clean
You know the type of bed I mean.
And as the world got slowly colder

She would climb in it and it would enfold her
A world of white and, in the distance could she hear
Singing? A voice she didn't know – but clear
Beautiful, female, pristine, far away.

In the distance Prudencia hears a woman's voice
singing 'Blackwaterside'.

And that's when the chairman turned to say –

Ms Hart – Ms Hart you have the floor.

— Mmmm?

You were saying?

— WHY DON'T YOU BELIEVE IN BEAUTY ANY MORE!

And on that surprise ejaculation
She blushed and finished her presentation.
Pause.
Desultory applause.

Desultory applause.

With a girlishly defeated frown
Prudencia Hart sat sadly down
Only to find her chair leg slip
Off the stage edge's wooden lip
And so she fell
Like Lucifer into Hell
And as she fell the audience mumbled
As if somehow the fact she tumbled
Upended her logically
As well as physically
And so as she landed tit under bum
It was a case of
Quod erat demonstrandum.
Pru was defeated – the debate was done
And Dr Colin Syme had won
Stupid Siolaigh and Professor Macintosh
Had defeated beauty – bish bash bosh.

FIVE

Colin and Prudencia.

Good debate.

— Was it? I didn't think it was that great.

You know – you take this stuff too seriously Pru.

— Do I?

Of course.
It's all . . . it's just talk – just discourse –
Your problem is you persist
Like – I don't know – some kind of romanticist
With a sort of old fashioned ethnographic notion of
    'collecting'
Or 'protecting'
Ballads – you know sometimes it seems
As if you genuinely think these memes
Are real.

— Don't you think they're real?

That depends what you think 'real' really means.

— Look Colin,
I have to go.

Wait, don't – stay and have a drink.
Some of us are going to the pub, I think.

— I want to get back to Edinburgh.

Come on, just one.

— I've got the car.

I've got the bike
C'mon.
One drink won't hurt – like.

23

— Why – so you can gloat?

Me gloat?

— I don't think so Colin, I'll get my coat.

Come on Pru have a drink – chew the fat – we only ever
meet at conferences.

— I wonder what the reason for that is.

I'll buy you dinner.
Slap-up nosh
A bottle of Chablis
Bish bash bosh.

— No.

OK so . . .
Bye.
Or do I mean
Au revoir.

Prudencia leaves. Colin follows.

— Bollocks.

What?

— Where the hell's my car?

Ah.

— Oh no.

Has it been stolen?

— It's been stolen
It's been stolen by snow.
I left it just there – before.

But now there's no there 'there' any more.
It's deep – what, six feet about?

— You have to help me dig it out.

What's the point – the roads will all be closed.

— There isn't a train station I don't suppose –

Shut – nineteen sixties – Beeching.

— Bollocks.

Don't worry.

— Don't worry? I'm supposed to be teaching.

Give the office a call – use my phone if you like.

— My poor little car.

My lovely bike.

— Maybe if we set off walking, while it's still light –

Prudencia, we're not going anywhere tonight.

SIX

So Colin Syme and Prudence Hart
Colleagues in the study of folk art
At the Edinburgh School of Scottish Studies
Colleagues – yes – but hardly buddies
Now were here – plumb stuck in Kelso
No bike – no car – no bus as well so
As Colin said:

We may as well see
If we can find a B and B.

— Where will we find one this late on?
Won't all the B and Bs have gone?

No problem, Prumeister – no worries, no fuss –
I'll find accommodation for both of us.

Prumeister – Prudence – Prudica – Pru –

25

UNIVERSITY OF WINCHESTER
LIBRARY

Was there no idiot nickname he wouldn't stoop to?

With that he took out his fancy mobile phone.
Prudencia thought – I might have known
He's always got the most up-to-date crap
A Bed-and-Breakfast-finding app!

Now Pru, Pru let me just set this thing
It scans the web and it gives me a ring
The moment it identifies a place it sees
Nearby my location with vacancies.
Enter numbers – a price – co-ordinates –
It'll phone me back in twenty minutes.
In the meantime I'm hungry – do you fancy some grub?

And with that he wandered over to a nearby pub
Sat low and grey in the market square
The sort of place that's always been there.

An olde-worlde sort of venue
With chalkboard signs displaying the menu
And underneath the bill of fare
Another chalk sign hanging there
That said in pink letters bold and clear
KELSO FOLK CLUB – FOLK NIGHT HERE!

— Wait – I'm coming with you –

And Prudencia went in.
The pub was quiet, it was early still
And the snow was up to the windowsill
But still – it really was very quiet
And Prudencia and Colin wondered why it
Was that there were only a few middle-aged blokes sitting
Round a table and a nice lady doing her knitting.
So they went over and asked the landlord
Who was busy writing out the menu board
Excuse me, we were just wondering –
Where's the session?

And here we make a small digression.

Prudencia saw a lot of sessions –
This one was far from being her first impression.
It was part of her work to travel for miles and miles
Recording different tunes, different players, different
    styles.
Prudencia had been in Highland village halls
And border cottages, and country balls
And one summer she was out virtually daily
Attending some or other ceilidh
So what Colin would call 'the signified'
– the concept or class of object implied
By the word 'session' was something like this:

> *Fiddles and banjos played with virtuosity and gusto.*

But looking now at the landlord pointing
Sessions in Kelso were disappointing,
In fact you might have thought he was taking the piss
Because this folk session looked like this.

> *Men sitting round a table playing Bob Dylan on
> acoustic guitar badly while looking at the words off
> photocopied song sheets.*

Jesus Christ. Do we have to stay?

— We don't know what they might do next – they might
    play
Some jigs or dances.

Look at them Prudencia, what are the chances?

— Oh, give it a chance Colin, it's still early.

This isn't desolation row this is prostate alley.

— Colin, these folk night sessions are informal,
Believe me this sort of thing is quite normal,
It's extremely likely that at any minute

Some real ballad singers will come along and take part
   in it.

Oh please, no, that's my idea of Hell – a
Middle-aged man singing *a capella*.

— Colin stay – it could be good –

I'm hungry – can we at least get some food?

— We'll order something, and till then there's bar snacks.
You know, the fiddles and the drums and clarsachs
And suchlike won't turn up till late.
This is just the warm-up it's only eight.
Colin, you know, we're in the Borders.
The real talent doesn't turn up till last orders.

Can I put on the juke box?

— No!

The telly?

— No! Colin I'm shocked –
Tonight we've got a chance to learn
Something – to turn
Inconvenience into chance for a real insight
Into the authentic folk expression of a Borders town on
   a winter's night.
Just try to sit still and see if you can
Increase your childish attention span.

OK.

— OK.

What do you want to drink?

— A pint of bitter.
What are you doing?

Checking Twitter.

The tune finishes.
   Applause.
   A man announces another tune.

Thanks, Derek – that was 'Bridge over Troubled Water'.
Now . . . Geoff . . . you're down to play 'The Earl of
   Rosslyn's Daughter'.

Oh, for fuck sake, Pru.

— What's wrong with you?

This song is shit and it takes fucking ages.

   The man plays.

Now, gents, forgive me, I know the chords but – Keith,
   can you turn the pages?

And so bold Colin struggled manfully
Not to fidget – while painfully
Geoff sang a song of seduction by the River Esk
His voice less Sandy Denny more Les Dawson-esque.
Two other bald men nodding along slowly
Geoff's cheap guitar strumming gently and lowly . . .
And then . . . at the quietest point of the tune
As a bald Geoff whispered his soul to the moon.

Suddenly –

   Colin's phone rings.

Colin's iPhone leapt into loud action –
Giving Prudence a bum-clenching pelvic contraction.

   Colin's ringtone is an Australian pop classic.

— Shhh!

Sorry – sorry!

Now Colin was the typical sort of a lad
Who'd have an iPhone or a Pod or a Pad.

He loved texts and texting and he used all the smilies
And if he had a ringtone – it would have to be Kylie's.

— For God's sake Colin!

What?

— That.

Oh – do you like it?

— Of course I don't like it – it's unbelievably crass.

How's it crass?

— Where do I start?

I suppose your ringtone is a recording of Anne Briggs
unaccompanied singing 'Willy o' Winsbury' recorded on
a beach in Knoydart?

— No it isn't.

Assynt?

— As a matter of fact, I don't have a ringtone at all.

Balls.

— My phone's set to vibrate.

Typical.

— What?

The middle-class vibrate – great.

— Middle-class?

Me crass. What about you – oh I'm so tasteful. I'm so . . .
  middlebrow.

— I have my phone on silent exactly for moments like
  this one now.
Very often I'm in the field recording
When people or playing or singing –

People who are in a special performing zone –
The last thing I want is for my mobile phone
To spoil a moment, so when I'm on the road.
I keep it set on silent mode.

How very ethnographic.

— What?

You're not on the road – you're stuck in traffic.

— Why do you have to be so yobbish?

Why do you have to be so snobbish?

   Colin's phone rings again.

Oh yes, hello. Tonight, yes. We'll take it. We'll take it –
great – thanks – cheers then.

— Well?

Good news. They have room.

— Great.

Just one.

— Bloody hell.

We could sleep top-to-toe.

— No.

I'll sleep on the floor, you can have the bed.

— Tell them no.

I've told them yes, I've already said.

— Bum.

Don't be glum –

And Prudencia looked around the room
At bald men moaning in the gloom

At Colin Syme beside her smiling slyly
On his iPhone downloading Kylie.
And Geoff . . . dull Geoff . . . croaking out the eighty-
    seventh verse.
She thought to herself . . .
I suppose things can't get any worse.

But they can.

Oh man.

They can.

The landlord rings a bell.

Ladies and Gentlemen –
It's Midwinter's Eve –
Can you sort out the microphone, Steve?
Call it solstice, call it Yule,
Call it the last day of term at school
Call it what you like – it's that moment when
We look back at the past then forward again
And then leap – jump over time's crack
Between looking forward and looking back,
A fractional second of universal still
When what 'was' is, and what is – is 'will'
And all time and everything stops
Even the ticking of the clocks
A midnight moment, when past and future kiss.
Midwinter.
Oh yes.
Without further ado
Let's get this party started!

Glitter ball, music, karaoke, noise.

And with a flourish of his bell and a shout
The landlord rubbed the chalk sign out.
And where it had said FOLK NIGHT HERE
It now said A POUND A PINT ALL BEER

And to complete the illiterate publicity
KARAOKE NITE! – spelt N–I–T–E.

*A troupe of four black crows mount the stage, all
feathers and glamour. They sing a weird karaoke.*

SEVEN

Ladies and gentlemen, we present the 'Ballad of the
   Four Corbies'.

*The corbies, hungover and exhausted, discuss their
night of debauchery [—* is the forgetful corbie
(crow, raven).]*

It was a good night.

It was a mad night.

It was a strange night.

Do you remember it?

—* No.

How could you forget it?

It's branded on the inside of my mind.

—* How could I remember it, I was plastered?

Carved.

It was epic.

—* I remember nothing.

The horror of it.

—* I tunnel into the recesses of my mind and I find
   nothing.

You're lucky.

Do you not even remember the flaming sambucca?

—* A big fat blank.

They were stacked up at the bar five glasses deep.

Like a fiery hell.

—* A blank as white as the snow that fell.

The four of us dressed all in red

As red as our own lipsticks.

A stain on the black night.

Red breath

Smeared against the steamy glass.

It was a mad night.

It was a great night.

It was a strange night.

It was like something out of Breughel.

The scotch-pie suppers.

—* The what?

Two each if I remember rightly.

—* Dear God, did we?

Salt and sauce and pickled eggs.

We fed the eggs to Geoff

Got him drunk.

—* Not Geoff – no.

And made him eat them one by one.

The breath on him when we kissed him.

—* We what?

It was part of the bet

Had he won or lost

He was our prize

Our slave.

We tied him up

With his own guitar strap

Naked

Except for a G-string.

—* I had no part in any of this.

Don't you remember?

—* No!

Lighting his breath with a lit sambucca?

—* No!

Like a steam engine pouring sparks out into the night
    as you sang to him

'I will always love you'

Scotch pie in your left hand microphone in your right

And in your mouth a big fat Havana cigar.

—* A cigar?

Don't you remember the cigars?

The scotch-pie suppers and the flaming sambucca and
the cigars?

—* I wondered why I was coughing up blood the next
morning.

It was a mad night.

It was a lovely night.

It was a strange night.

It was like something out of Pasolini.

Geoff the sex slave, the Cuban cigars, the scotch-pie suppers, the flaming sambucca, and the explicit strip.

—* The what?

You stripped.

—* I did?

You.

You got up on that table there

And you took your clothes off.

Every last stitch.

—* I did not.

Don't you remember?

—* I refuse to accept.

Geoff was tied to the karaoke machine

Singing James Blunt.

'You're beautiful'

In his best contralto

His tie around his testicles.

We were transported.

'You're beautiful'

And you got up.

—* I got up?

A tear in your eye.
—* Oh God.
And you wobbled
—* Dear Lord.
Up on to the table
—* Please no more.
'You're beautiful'
And you had a flaming sambucca in one hand
And a cigar in the other
Geoff's underpants on your head
'You're beautiful'
And you stripped.
The whole bar sang
'You're beautiful'
Stripped
Right
Down
To
Your
Thong.
—* So wrong.
Lay back
On the bar
Legs in the air

Like an upturned cow

And to roars of applause

You kicked the scotch pie off the table.

—* Dear God.

It was a good night.

It was a mad night.

It was a strange night.

It was like something out the Marquis de Sade.

—* So let's recap – there was Geoff the sex slave, the stripping, the flaming sambuccas, the scotch-pie suppers, the cigars – was there anything else?

Nothing.

—* You're sure?

Sure.

Well – there was the boy.

—* The boy?

The boy from the country-clothing store.

—* Oh no.

Oh yes.

—* Did we?

We did.

—* All three of us?

All three of us.

—* That wee boy?

That wee boy.

—* That poor wee laddie?

That poor wee laddie.

— * The one with the limp?

The limp and the tousled hair and –

—* The slight look of fearfulness?

The slight look of fearfulness.

—* Where?

In the ladies.

—* All of us?

All of us.

—* One at a time or as an ensemble?

One at a time.

And as an ensemble.

—* I don't remember.

I can't forget.

—* So there was the flaming sambuccas, the scotch-pie suppers, the cigars, the stripping, Geoff the sex slave, the boy from the country-clothing store and nothing else.

Nothing.

Well.

Only the gulling of the lassie.

—* The gulling?

Yes.

—* Oh, I remember that.

 Prudencia in her coat, buttoned up.

Karaoke all around.
The harpies assail her.

What did she say your name was?

— Prudencia.

What?

— PRUDENCIA.

What?

— It doesn't matter.

You don't look like you're enjoying yourself, Prudencia.

— No, I'm fine.

We wondered if you wanted cheering up, Prudencia.

We wanted to get you into the swing of things, Prudencia.

— I'm really having a lot of fun.

Are you sure?

— I actually enjoy this sort of thing really a lot.

Would you like a flaming sambucca?

— No.

Would you like a bite of scotch pie?

— No.

Would you like a cigar?

— No.

Would you like to strip?

— NO!

Are you from Edinburgh, Prudencia?

— Yes.

Poor thing.

That explains it.

The shyness.

People from Edinburgh are famous for being shy.

They don't like to reveal themselves.

Very proper.

But underneath

There's a blood-red heart bursting like a sack full of
snakes

Isn't that right?

— What?

Isn't an Edinburgher's heart underneath all that propriety

Perpetually half-present at an orgy

Of drink and sex and blasphemy?

Isn't that what they say about Edinburgh folk?

— Well, I don't know.

Come on, you and me – let's get on the table and we'll
do a wee strip – it'll be hilarious. Come on . . . it's warm
in here.

— I'll just keep my coat on if that's OK.

You know your problem?

— I really don't have a problem. I just think –

Prudencia

You're over-dressed

You need to unpeel

41

The way to cope with cold.

Is to let it touch

Your naked skin

Show the world you're not afraid of it.

— Actually, you know, that's a common misconception but all the medical evidence suggests that drunk people who venture out unprepared in winter end up lying in the snow in their underwear dying of hypothermia –

Evidence?

Prudencia.

Have you ever heard of the law of opposites?

If you're tired – dance.

If it's raining – swim.

Whatever it is you want, Prudencia, the opposite is always the answer

What is it that you want, Prudencia?

— I'm actually surprisingly tired. I really think I want to go to bed.

Then it's decided.

Stay.

It's the only way.

The door slams.

THAT'S A LOCK-IN LADIES AND GENTLEMEN, IT'S HALF PAST ELEVEN AND PAST TIME, IF YOU LEAVE NOW YOU DON'T GET BACK IN. THAT'S A LOCK-IN. THAT'S A LOCK-IN.

Besides

You can't go out there alone tonight
Not tonight.

Why not?

Tonight's the night of the Devil's Ceilidh.

— The Devil's Ceilidh?

That's right.

— What's the Devil's Ceilidh?

FOOTNOTE TO THE 3RD EDITION

The Devil's Ceilidh is a dance or party hosted by Satan and reputed to be held at exactly midnight on the winter solstice (Cunningam, 1976, p. 42), when a gap or gate opens up in time. The Devil roams abroad and human souls can be taken down to Hell before their time. The Devil hosts his Ceilidh with the intention of luring souls, usually maidens, into his trap.

— Goodness.

So you see.

You'd have to stay.

And you have to sing.

— No honestly!

Come on.

Everybody else has sung.

It's your turn

It's your turn for a turn, Prudencia.

We want your song.

Everybody's given a piece of themselves

Except you.

Come on –

What's your song?

'Dear Prudence?'

'We are Family'?

Uptight?

Or is it . . .

'*Je t'aime moi non plus*'?

Which song is yours, Prudencia?

Which one's you?

SING! SING! SING! SING!

— I don't have a bloody song!

Prudencia runs to the toilets.

All cry 'Prudencia!'

— Leave me alone.

Prudencia reaches the Ladies. Laughter from the harpies.

—* So – in summary – there was the flaming sambuccas, the scotch-pie suppers, Geoff the sex slave, the cigars, the cocaine, the stripping and the boy from the country-clothing store and the gulling of the lassie, and was there any more?

No.

That was the end of it.

From the chaos of the night, somehow

We conjured a conclusion

Spontaneous

And

Colourful

And

Cathartic

—* What was it?
This apt ending we made for ourselves?

We boaked.

There was a bit of enforced bulimia in the Ladies

Fingers down throats

And everything that had gone in came out

All the singing and smoking

All the drinking and the talking

All the stripping and the fighting

And the slaving and the psalming

All that which was

That which had been

The past

Came roaring back up from down below.

And impressed itself upon the present.

Up up up and out it came

In waves

In choruses

Unstoppable as a song

Until it lay splattered all over the lavatory bowl

Like

A poem

About a really good night out.

EIGHT

The sounds of the party come muffled through the toilet walls.

Hiding in the toilet like a schoolgirl
Prudencia's heart was a nauseous whirl
Of self-disgust at her own inability
To participate, the perpetual social disability
Which had her always stood outside observing
Like an emotional voyeur perving
At other people's grief or joy or lust – intent
On capturing a transcendent moment
And setting it in stone
While always feeling herself alone.

Prudencia felt drunk and sad.
It had been a while since she had felt this bad.
Looking in the mirror in the Ladies
She felt her soul fall into Hades
Like a spiralling leaf from an autumn branch
Or the moment just before an avalanche
The sudden dark groan of grief
The snow releases in relief
At no longer having to hide
Its inability to cling to a mountainside.
Like a great falling down of snow
Prudencia felt herself let go.

When a character's feelings are like the weather
We call it 'pathetic fallacy', but whatever
Do we call it when
Electricity mirrors a character's emotion?
Electric fallacy? Synecdoche? I don't know what
But suddenly there was a power cut.

    A power cut.
      All goes quiet.

All light candles.

The dark caught everyone unawares
But not Prudencia – 'not that anyone cares'
She thought, with weary pride
'But once a girl guide always a girl guide.'

   Prudencia takes out a head torch from her handbag.

Spiral leaves, rain, souls slowly falling
Colin drunk outside the toilet calling
Pru thought to herself – there's only one thing I really
   know,
When you feel this crap at a party, it's time to go.

At which sad moment fate drew her eye
To something on the lavvy wall close by
Cards for taxis, pizzas and, no, just slight concealed,
A card for the B and B at Goodman's Field.

NINE

Prudencia stepped out into the cold night air
Prepared yet unprepared
Propelled from a room full of sex, song and violence
Into a world of utter silence.

   Prudencia checks the map on the back of the card.

— Left then left then left again.
OK.

Walk.

Cold.

Moon.

Blue

Night

47

Bright.

— Left, then left, then left again.

Tear

Star

Fear

Car

Park

Dark

Breath

— Left, then left, then left again.

Street

Black

Blank

Stone

Alley

Square.

Maybe there's somebody there.

— Hello?

Step

Step

Step

Stop.

— Hello?

Walk

Breathe

Frost

Fast

Fear

Forest

Night.

— This can't be right.

Dog

Fence

Owl

Moon

Cloud.

Shh . . .

— I can hear my own heart beat out loud.

Prudencia takes out her mobile phone. She dials the number on the B and B card.

— Hello . . . hello my name's Prudencia Hart. I believe I have a booking with you. I'm . . . look, I'm sorry it's late . . . It's just about ten to twelve and I'm trying to find you. I think I might be lost. I've come out of the town and down a riverside walkway into some sort of forest and . . . according to your card I should be here but . . . anyway I wonder if you could call me back on –

Beeeeeeeeep.

— Bollocks.

No

One

No

Sign

No

Light

No

Heat

No

Soul

Alone

And

No

Reception.

— Fuck.

She scrabbled up the riverbank through the trees
Pulling on bushes on her hands and knees.
Finally she emerged on to a patch of ground
Desolate, desperate, resigned to her fate
She looked round
And found
She was in some kind of housing estate
Rows of grey homes all pebble-dashed
Gardens with sofas in, bus shelters trashed
And the whole place empty – no one about
No footprints in the snow even – all trace wiped out
By fresh snow – Pru supposed.
Even the Asian grocery shop was closed
No lights in any windows, one sodium lamp
Flickered and buzzed on and off in the damp
Night air and Prudencia was about to turn and go
When she saw, suddenly, a woman – standing in the

orange glow.
Evanescent she seemed – as if she were made
Of breath. All around her small children played,
Toddlers, a baby, the oldest ten at most
Silent and as pale as ghosts
Like creeping plants they climbed and clung on to their
    mother,
Sister climbed on sister, brother on brother,
And in the middle of it all, still and white,
The woman from the estate – singing to the night.

TEN

The Woman from the Estate sings.

SONG: BLACKWATERSIDE

One morning fair I took the air
Down by Blackwaterside
Was in gazing all around me
'Twas the Irish lad I spied.

All through the far part of the night
We rolled in sport and play
Then the young man rose and put on his clothes
Saying fare thee well today.

That's not the promise that you made to me
When you lay upon my breast
You made me believe with your lying tongue
That the sun rose in the west.

Go home, go home to your father's garden
Go home and cry your fill
And think of your own misfortune
You brought on by your wanton will.

There's not a girl in this wide world

So easily led as I
Sure when fishes do fly and seas do run dry
It is then you will marry I.

One morning fair as I took the air
Down by Blackwaterside
Was in gazing all around me
'Twas the Irish lad I spied.

*Children climb all around the Woman. They hiss at
Prudencia.*

— Excuse me – excuse me, hello?
I'm looking for Goodman's Field?
It's a bed and breakfast.
Do you know it?

The Woman nods.

— Could you tell me how to get there?
Only . . . it's late and I'm supposed to be staying there.
Well, I'm booked in.

Don't go.

— Sorry?

Stay.

— I'm booked in.

It's late
We've got a mattress on the floor.

— It's kind but – I can't impose.

Stay.
It's late.
I'll make up a bed on our floor
And give you tea
We have chips
And a heater.

We can watch television together
I have a bottle of vodka.
I have half a carton of cigarettes
And I have a photograph album
Full of pictures of the children when they were babies.
Stay.

— Gosh. I'm overwhelmed.

Stay.

— Thank you, but
. . .
But maybe if you can just give me a quick pointer so
I can orientate myself I'll be on my way –

Left, left, then left again.

The Woman from the Estate disappears.

ELEVEN

Left and left again took Prudencia back to where
She'd started off in the old town square
In the grey stone pub – the lights still burning
Where the lock-in party was now turning
Into some kind of hellish bacchanal,
An upturned midwinter festival
Of heat and light and naked flesh
In stark contrast to the pure white fresh
World of the snow here outside
Where in the dark Prudencia could hide
And – as is her habit – watch
As the pull of alcohol and crotch
Absorbed these disparate souls into a single one-ness
Of sex and song and drink and fun-ness.
Here a drunk and a naked banshee
Brandishing a cigar, no – can she?

Yes, she can, and who's with her – Siolaigh
Dancing with Colin, no you don't say,
And in the firelight who's that older man
Playing the spoons and banging a can?
It's Professor Macintosh – and so a quorum
Colin, Siolaigh and the Prof all indecorum.
Prudencia was cold and tired and weary
The streets of Kelso felt empty, eerie,
As she watched her colleagues fall to into sin
She wondered if she should go back in.

>*The midnight bell tolls.*
>>*At each strike we see a flash picture of the*
>*debauchery going on inside the pub.*
>>*Man spikes drink with Rohypnol.*
>>*Woman gives man a Prince Albert in his cock.*
>>*Spit-roasting Siolaigha.*
>>*Glue-sniffing.*
>>*Etc.*

>*Prudencia watches it all in horror.*

>*The last bell.*
>>*Silence.*

Prudencia?

>*She gasps in fright.*

I'm Nick, from Goodman's field?

— I'm sorry – I . . .

You rang.

— Oh – yes.

You said you were lost.

— You're from the B and B.

I thought I'd come and find you.

— Oh God, you gave me such a fright.

I'm sorry.

— It's OK. I'm just – glad to see you.

Good.

— How did you find me?

Footprints in the snow.

— Of course, I never thought, stumbling about in the snow

You leave traces.

. . .

And, of course, I recognised you.

— You recognised me.

From the conference.

— I don't remember you.

I came in late, I sat at the back.

— Are you – I'm sorry – have we met?

I don't think so, have we?

— You seem familiar.

So do you.

— Are you in Folk Studies?

Not professionally but – it's a subject I have an interest in. I have a lot of time on my hands. I like to spend it in . . . what you might call self-improvement. When I saw there was a conference on the ballads – a subject about which I'm passionate – I thought I'd go along. You spoke very well.

— It was embarrassing.

You were the only speaker who made any sense.

— It's kind of you to say that, but I think these days you're in the minority.

Idiocy is idiocy, whether it's voiced by the majority or not.

— The thing that's so frustrating is that I've devoted my life to studying these stories. These ballads aren't – discourses to me – they're not – processes or sociological artefacts . . . they're art. I don't study them to . . . diminish them, I study them because . . . they contain something elusive –

Something beyond the words themselves.

— That's it.

Something eternal.

— Exactly.

Something you want to capture.

— Yes.

You know.

I'm a collector too.
. . .
You must be cold.

— A little.

There's a warm fire waiting for you.

— Thank you.

Unless, of course, you'd rather stay here.

— His eyes were dark – he smiled politely.
'It's up to you,' he said, and she felt slightly
Afraid of him, this man who stepped so lightly
On the snow that, as he walked into the dark,

She noticed that his footsteps left no mark.

— Wait, I'm coming.

TWELVE

She followed him through the pale blue light
Of a snowbound, moonlit, Borders night
Where before she'd been struggling, tired
Prudencia felt awake now, wired,
Because despite – or because of – his eccentricity
This man Nick seemed to radiate electricity.

It's not far. Just past Asda.

As he strode the deserted car park
She saw something flicker in his eyes, a spark?
Was it possible to radiate light? She didn't know.
Was it the moon? – she thought – or did he actually glow?

Here we are.

He pointed to
An unprepossessing modern bungalow.

Prudencia's heart sank –

Three flying ducks hung on the wall
Of the flock-wallpapered hall
A painting of the stag at bay
Jigsaws for the guests to play
Tartan upholstery and an extremely grand
Elephant's foot umbrella stand.

Chez moi, my humble home, *entrez, mam'selle*.

Prudencia sighed, this B and B was her idea of Hell.

Would you like a nightcap?

— I'm not sure.

She hesitated –

His glow she liked but his décor she hated.

I'll open a malt whisky?
Let's sit by the fire, in the library.

— You have a library?

Nothing special, really,
Just a small collection.
Mostly manuscripts that interest me.
Folk.
Poetry.
Ballads.

— Prudencia's ears pricked up, like a fox's,
Now this was ticking all her boxes.

Would you like to see?

— Yes, that would be nice.

With a smile, he opened the door
To

— Paradise.

Prudencia stared into the firelit gloom
Slack-jawed at the sheer size of the room
Forty feet tall and an acre wide
Books lining the walls on every side.

— It's huge.

I did have to convert the garage.

— There must be thousands of books in here.

Just over a hundred thousand, I think.

— Have you read them all?

Most of them.

— Oh. My. God.

Have you found something you like?

— You have an original Whitelaw!
And a first edition of the *Minstrelsy*
Signed!
The Proceedings of the Society of Antiquaries of Scotland
Volumes one to eleven.

So what do you think?

— It's . . . just . . . heaven.

I think so too.

— I could stay here forever.

It's funny you should say that.

— Why?

I was thinking you might stay a little longer than one night.

— Oh.

Prudencia.
I'm alone.
I have a little trouble sleeping.
It would be nice to have some company.

— I can't.

You can.

— I have to teach.

Not any more.

Prudencia felt the tiniest tightening of fear,
She wasn't sure what was going on here.

— You know what? It's late, I think maybe I'll go to bed.

59

UNIVERSITY OF WINCHESTER
LIBRARY

It's locked.

She turned – and clocked
The fire reflected in his eye.

Prudencia, we have a lot in common, you and I.

Each of us alone, and questing
To capture that which we find interesting.
To fix the butterfly with a pin
To catch a thought with words to put it in,
We don't have such different roles
It's just –
You're a collector of songs, and I'm a collector of souls.

She looked at him in the armchair, sat
Feet curled up under him like a cat
His expression catlike, yearning and aloof
But where a cat has paws – he had – a hoof.

Sudden blowing out of candles.

Part the Second

ONE

In the Library: the Devil and Prudencia.

— Right
I don't –
Just to be clear.
Because –
Hell?
And you're –

Yes.

— I don't believe you.

It doesn't matter what you believe.

Right – no . . . Because I study these things – I'm the
Scottish expert on Hell, and – it's – it's – well, whatever
it is – it's not a B and B.

It is a *weird* B and B.

— No!

Midwinter.
Midnight.
Full moon.
A stranger.
What on earth did you expect would happen?

— This is not Hell. You are not the Devil. This is not a
ballad. I am in a Bed and Breakfast just outside Kelso
and you are a nutter – sorry but – at least – a sufferer
from mental illness – at any rate – I don't know who you
are and now I'm going to take my phone out of my pocket
and call . . . the . . . police – stay back!

The phone is dead.

— Shit.

You're funny.

— Am I?

I never know who I'm going to get on these midwinter's nights. Usually it's an idiot. Some drunk lad stumbling home from the pub. But you're not an idiot, are you, Prudencia?

— Right – that's it – that's enough – I get it now – flattery – hooves – I'm dreaming. My subconscious is bound to be steeped in the particulars of supernatural imagery – like – like – so what's happening here is a dream and these images are playing out inside my subconscious in order for me to work out some inner problem – almost certainly sexual. Right now I'm almost certainly lying in the snow, drunk, and hypothermic – I knew I shouldn't have had that flaming Sambucca. Wake up! Wake up!

You're funny.

A croaked scream.
    She closes her eyes.
    She croaks.
    She opens her eyes.

— Are you going to kill me?

I already have.

A moment.
    He pours a drink.

Would you like a drink?

He offers.
    She takes it.

Cheers.

She throws the drink in his face.

Welcome to Hell. Make yourself at home. You'll find there's plenty for you to occupy your time: there's jigsaws and you can watch the rain fall on the Asda car park and of course there's the library. Every book there's ever been is here, and every book there's never been as well. There's also a pretty extensive collection of rare vinyl. Explore, take your time, you have an eternity. Breakast is served from 7.0 till 8.30, dinner at 9.0 and I'm always happy to provide packed lunches . . . as long as you let me know . . . the night before.

He holds the drink out to her.

— Help.

. . .

HELP!

. . .

HELP!

. . .

Help.

> *She takes the drink.*
> *She falls.*
> *She falls through years . . .*
> *Years and years pass.*
> *She falls from rejection of her surroundings to curiosity about them.*
> *She is caught.*

TWO

Prudencia listening to a record. The Devil watches her.

This is nice.

> *A distant, crackly, voice sings 'My Love is Like a Red Red Rose'.*

— Nice? It's Robert Burns.

Oh.

— It's *sung* by Robert Burns. That's Burns's own voice. In a pub in Mauchline in 1829. I found it under a pile of manuscripts of lectures by Hume in a box labelled 'Pornographic Etchings'. There's so much stuff here I don't know where to start.

Everything that ever was is here. It doesn't matter where you start.

— You should really have a catalogue.

Why?

— I could have missed this.

You'd have found it in the end.

— How do you know?

There is no end.

— You should have a catalogue.

> *Beat.*
> *She falls through years.*
> *Years and years*
> *She falls from wild curiosity into a routine of work.*
> *She is caught.*

THREE

How are you getting on?

— I think I'm about a third way through.

It's been a thousand years.

— These things take time.

By the way, I've been meaning to ask.

What?

— I wonder if you wouldn't mind knocking.

Knocking?

— Before you just suddenly appear.

Sorry.

— It's been getting on my nerves.

I have to adopt a form.

— Well, couldn't you at least knock before you materialise. I could have been doing anything.

What could you have been doing?

— Anything.

You said you could have been doing anything.

— I don't know, something private.

Like what?

— I don't know.

What?

— You know.

I don't.

— You may not have a bodily form, but I do.

Oh that!

— Yes that.

I've seen that.

— Oh.

Many times.

Wouldn't you – if you were in my shoes?

  . . .

Bear in mind I know the answer.

> *She falls through years.*
> *Years and years.*
> *She falls from awkward formality to being totally*
> *completely unselfconsciously at home.*
> *She is caught.*

FOUR

Prudencia reads a dusty old book.

Lady Eliot of Broughton – thirteenth-century diary – it's
never been seen before – no one knew it even existed – I
mean it needs editing – quite apart from the background
detail about life in a Borders hall — I was actually
wondering about editing it myself. Listen to this – 17th
February 1269. 'Visiting singer from Selkirk. Ralph. He
gave us twa sangs – "Lord Ranald" and a new sang of
his own composing – "The Border Widow's Lament".'
See?
The 'Border Widow's Lament'.
A song.
Not a discourse.
Composed.
Dated.
Take that, Professor Macintosh.
Shove that in your late-capitalist pipe and smoke it.
I was right.
I was right.

  . . .

What?

— Nothing.

What?

— It doesn't matter, does it?

No.

— None of it matters.

> *She falls through the years.*
> *Years and years.*
> *She falls away from work into boredom.*
> *She is caught.*

FIVE

She looks out of the window.

What are you looking at?

— The grass growing through the cracks in the tarmac in the Asda car park.

> *She falls through the years.*
> *She falls through years and years.*
> *She falls from stillness to stillness.*
> *She is caught.*

SIX

She looks through the window.

— An aspen grew up through one of the disabled spaces. As it grew it pushed a stone up from the earth. This morning a dog came out of the forest. It walked across to the tree. It sniffed the stone and licked it. The tree shivered.

It's very hot.

— Is it?

Perhaps there was water on it.

— Perhaps.

. . .

I wanted to be that dog so much.

> *She falls through the years.*
> *Through years and years.*
> *She falls from stillness into despair.*
> *She is caught.*

SEVEN

*The Devil and Prudencia dance. The Devil sings 'My
Love is Like a Red Red Rose'.*

— I want to go home.

> *She falls through the years.*
> *She falls through years and years.*
> *She falls from despair to desperate energy.*
> *She is caught.*

EIGHT

Prudencia throws herself at the window.
> *And again.*
> *And again.*
> *The Devil catches her every time.*

— You must be tired.

I'm fine.

— Don't you ever sleep?

No.

— Even when you're not with me?

Busy busy busy.

— I don't know how you manage it.

It's not so bad.

— You look tired.

I'm fine.

— Your eyes are lined.

Not my eyes.

— No?

I have no bodily form.

— You seem prickly.

I'm not prickly.

— Why don't you dematerialise?

I'm fine.

— When you adopt a form you forget that forms bring
with them needs. Bodily form needs food and you've
been in that form for the last seven years. I've barely
seen you eat.

I'm not prickly.

— Perhaps you have low blood sugar.

I'm not prickly except in so far as you are going on at
me for being prickly.

— I'm not going on at you. I'm just saying –

You're not 'just saying' anything.
You're trying to divert attention from the issue in hand.

— Which is?

Every time you try to escape I will catch you.

— You'll lose concentration.

Never.

— Just once.

I never lose concentration. I never sleep.

— No rest for the wicked.

No rest for the wicked.

> *She falls through the years.*
> *She falls through years and years.*
> *She falls from realisation to research.*

NINE

Candles.
> *Aromatherapy oils.*
> *Ambient music.*
> *Prudencia gives the Devil a massage.*

— I'm getting a lot of knots in your back.

I know. I ought to stretch more.

— Your shoulders are very tight.

Work.

— Let it go.

Sometimes I just want to – I don't know – give up –
slough off the infinite core of being and I don't know –
become a market gardener somewhere – you know –
concentrate on simple physical work – vegetables –
maybe chickens – but it wouldn't work – I'd get bored –
time would unroll before me and inevitably I'd become
an evil gardener – an evil *immortal* gardener and before
you know it Hell would be an allotment . . .

70

— Let it all go.

I wish I could.

— You can.

I can't.

— Shh.

I'd better go.

— Stay.

I'd better go.

He goes.

She falls through the years.
Years and years.
He falls alone, she watches him.
She is caught.

TEN

The Devil returns.

— Hello.

Hello.

— You were away a long time.

Was I?

— Four hundred years.

I didn't notice.

— I watched you.
Sitting under the aspen tree.
Perched on that stone.
Looking into the woods.

I was thinking.

— What were you thinking about?

Nothing.

— I missed you.

I'd better go.

— Don't.

ELEVEN

— There's a book missing.

Is there?

— *The Topography of Hell in Scottish Balladry.*

I don't know that one.

— My PhD.

Maybe one of the other guests borrowed it.

— Maybe.
Which is why it's lucky that it was quoted at length in
Border Ballads Neither Borders nor Ballads: Discuss!

She opens it.

— 'Dedicated to the Memory of Our Dear Friend and
Colleague Prudencia Hart.'

A moment.

— In it we find a paper from Dr Colin Syme – 'The
Pastoral Tradition as Expressed in Modern Terrace
Culture, or "Sheep Shagging Bastards"'. He quotes from
my PhD:

Prudencia quotes from a book.

'It's interesting that folk representations of Hell are often accompanied by the idea of the Devil forming a powerful erotic attachment for his human captive. In this sense we might say that the topography of Hell is also the topography of unrequited love.'

That's quite ridiculous.

— Is it?

We're in Hell.
Love is impossible.

— It happens in ballads.

This is not a ballad.

— Not yet.

> *She touches him, he moves away.*
> *A very long silence.*

You're funny.

— What would happen if we talked in rhyme?

> *She moves towards him.*

Well, I must be going – is that the . . . hour.

— Don't go, my dear, my darling – flower
Of my heart.

> *She moves towards him.*

Now look Prudencia, don't you sta— begin.

— Whenever I come near you – you change your form –

Formlessness is more the norm–al thing for me.

— That's right, in fact all this time we've existed in prose
Which is interesting
Because – as every author knows –
If you surrender your thought to metre

73

You surrender yourself to the poem's beat, or
Rhyme or formula or words or sound.
The author is lost and creation found,
The poem finds itself – its own *autonomia* –

Where are you going with this, Prudencia?

— What happens if we let go of prose?

We can't –

— Why not? If we adopt a more poetic form, who knows
What might happen?
The tighter the form the less control
We have over meaning or, you might say, soul.

You can't just throw ideas together like some sort of
    intellectual fruit salad.
You're real, I'm real, we're in Hell, Prudencia – not in a
    border – poem . . .

— Don't you see, your lonely discontent
Only exists because of your authorial intent,
Your determination to show love's impossibility.
But what if love's not impossible in poetry?
What happens if we both give up? – Let
Go? Give ourselves over to the rhyming couplet?

I have to go.

— Please – no.

  He hesitates.
    She tries to touch him again.
    Again he evades her.

— Long ago, in Kelso –
I don't know if I told you this or not?
Something happened that I've never forgot.
Four frightening women with enormous tits
Taught me the rule of opposites.
So now let's ask ourselves what does that rule tell

Two people trapped for an eternity in Hell
With a satanic loneliness so unbearably deep
Locked in on itself and unable to sleep?

I don't know.

— Well, if you want to strip a lover
First you must yourself uncover
And if that's true with clothes it's true with a heart.
If you want one opened up, first start
By opening up your own, let fall
A gap where once there was a wall.

She moves his body – so it moves with hers.

— Let go of words – move.

Prudencia what are you trying to prove?

— Let's be like a couple at the bar
Who don't even notice the way they are
Turning together to pick up a sandwich
Unconsciously copying each other's body language.

Maybe we should just discuss folk?

— Fuck folk.

She moves to him.
   They fall through the years.
   Through years and years.
   They fall into one.
   They are undone.
   She is caught.

TWELVE

Prudencia wakes up.
   The Devil is asleep in her arms.
   She extracts herself carefully, so as not to wake him up.

She looks out of the window.
She looks at him, asleep, peaceful.

— I love you,
But even love's made Hell
By immortality.

She takes the key from the Devil's belt.

I'll miss you, Devil,
I wonder if you'll miss me.

She leaves.
The Devil opens his eyes.
He is alone.

Prudencia?

Prudencia?

He realises she has gone.

NO!

The Devil's eyes go red.
Blood falls from his fingertips.
Smoke comes from his mouth.

THIRTEEN

You know the way you lose your sight –
When you step from darkness into light?
Your unaccustomed eyes finding
Even the palest moonlight blinding?
Well, imagine having been – not exactly sightless –
But lifeless – worldless – sensationless – light-less
For several millennia.
Now then, imagine how the world seemed
To Prudencia
When she stepped out into that earthly night.

Midwinter, midnight, moon full, snow white.

Imagine the pain of a frozen plant in spring –
The moment when it can't stop the season forcing
Heat up through cold roots – water turning
To fire – every frozen vein and vessel burning –
Every cell a sudden furnace of white-hot life.
That's how Prudencia felt – that night – a knife
Of heat plunged into a world of ice.
She was in pain – but it was nice.
Overwhelmed by sensation – stood stock still
She watched her breath form clouds until –

PRUDENCIA!

His cold voice froze the sap, the juice of her
She saw him now – not Nick but Lucifer.
Monstrous he clawed the empty air and screamed a yell
That tore apart the very fabric of Hell.
His eyes grew red, his claws dripped blood,
His mouth became a drooling flood
Of noxious smoke and fire and pitch,
He roared and cried –

   The Devil has transformed into a bear man.

DON'T LEAVE ME ALL ALONE – YOU BITCH!

For once she didn't have a plan.
Instinct took over and she just – just – fucking – ran.

FOURTEEN

I'm through, thought Pru, and at last she saw –

The crack in time – time's open door.
A pale slash in the fabric of the universe
Not unlike the graphic in the Silk Cut adverts.
Pru leapt towards it – a hunted hind,

77

Her hunter running close behind
Through the forest – and over the grass
And on to the car park and – 'Oh shit bugger arse,'
She remembered with a chill of fright
To escape Hell – a fair maid always needs a knight
Knight as in knight with a kicking-k,
Not night the opposite of day.
A knight errant or otherwise on a white horse
To pull the maiden from the Devil's grip with knightly
    force.
A lovesick warrior with a helmet and sword,
A chivalric lover with a way with a word.
But what chance did Prudencia have – do you think?
As she raced towards the midnight gap – the chink
Between the mighty walls of time –
Where past and future kiss – to find a knight?
No chance at all, to be quite frank – 'Shite.'
She reached out through the crack in the dark
Into the cold emptiness of the car park
In hopeless hope in – in desperate fear.
Could her hand find the hand of a chevalier?

HELP! HELP! IS ANYBODY THERE!
I NEED A HAND!

Prudencia!

The Devil bore down fast upon her
Pru could feel his breath upon her
LEG!

> *The Devil grabs Prudencia's leg.*
> *Prudencia screams.*

Poor Pru – no knight this night.

No luck this time, unless . . .

> *A voice in the darkness.*

Colin – Pru, over here.

It isn't, it can't be –

Prudencia It's Colin Syme.

ONE COLIN SYME
THERE'S ONLY ONE COLIN SYME
ONE COLIN SY – IME
THERE'S ONLY ONE COLIN SY – IME.

FIFTEEN

Ladies and gentlemen, we present the Ballad of Co Lin.

It would be lovely if you could join in.

It's not exactly a ballad it's mair a

Football chant to the tune of 'Guantanamera'.

ONE COLIN SYME
THERE'S ONLY ONE COLIN SYME
ONE COLIN SY – IME
THERE'S ONLY ONE COLIN SY – IME.

Kelso pub! Midwinter! Session! Orgy.

Uproar! Depravity! Karaoke.

And in the middle of it – tall as a horse

And as handsome as a lamp post

Colin Syme at the microphone.

Colin's karaoke fills the flesh-hungry bar

Tom Jones crossed with Barry White.

With a dash of Jay-Z and some Lady Gaga

Holding the mike like Darth Vader's lightsaber.

UNIVERSITY OF WINCHESTER
LIBRARY

Sex Colin sings and all women fall for him.

Women of Haddon and Roxburgh and Lempitlaw

Women of Maxwellheugh, Smailholm and Makerstoun

Women of and Stichill and Sprouston and Trows

All the women of Kelso on both sides the Tweed

Cheer Sex Colin singing and as he sings – strip him.

ONE COLIN SYME
THERE'S ONLY ONE COLIN SYME
ONE COLIN SY – IME
THERE'S ONLY ONE COLIN SY – IME.

Colin (*sings*)
  'In the jungle the mighty jungle
  The lion sleeps tonight.'

Oh desire of Kelso – a great sigh of wanting-ness

Rolling towards him a hot mist of pheromones

But up on the table top – Star Colin is standing

Troubled – a sentinel – alert – uneasy

Like Ronaldo the night of the World Cup Final

Like Zapruder filming the president's motorcade

Like Elvis alone on the lavatory straining –

Colin Syme senses that something is wrong.

Something is wrong or someone is missing

Because singer and sexer is not all Colin Syme is.

He's fighter and scholar and he's Colin Syme, Lover

With a heart as tender as Delia's slow-cooked beef.

On the outside insensitive – tough as old leather –

But cut Colin open and inside his chest find

Deep in amongst the blood and the offal

Nesting.

Like a baby bird.

One word.

'Prudencia'.

ONE COLIN SYME
THERE'S ONLY ONE COLIN SYME
ONE COLIN SY – IME
THERE'S ONLY ONE COLIN SY – IME.

Oh Colin beneath your bluster and bravado

Beats the heart of a bewildered wee student

Sitting at a window one hot day in summer

Dreaming of the girl he saw at the Proclaimers gig

A still point – serene – in a sweet summer frock.

Down at his feet fawned all Kelso's womanhood.

But for all that borderland female fecundity

All Colin could see was an absence – a blankness.

Where there should be Prudencia no Prudencia was there.

So down went the microphone – Bold Colin dropped it.

Don't go Colin – no! – cried the women of Lempitlaw.

As out through the calling crowd Colin walked swiftly.

Out into the night so sweetly to save her –

PRUDENCIA!

ONE COLIN SYME
THERE'S ONLY ONE COLIN SYME
ONE COLIN SY – IME
THERE'S ONLY ONE COLIN SY – IME.

Kelso is icy but fearless of cold – I am

Hercules – Finn Machuill – I am Samuel L. Jackson

Striding the bridge over the Tweed – Kelso bound up so white.

Tighter than Kylie's dress spread across her white thighs.

See me, bold Col-meister striding so gallant

A gallanter Syme you never did see

Atop my proud head – a bonny gay helmet

My testicles protected by proud Calvin Kleins

My insides are hot with Jack Daniels and Diet Coke

In my proud gallant fist a bonny gay sword

Well – not a bonny gay sword exactly but a bonny gay cocktail stick

In the shape of a sword.

ONE COLIN SYME
THERE'S ONLY ONE COLIN SYME
ONE COLIN SY – IME
THERE'S ONLY ONE COLIN SY – IME.

Down through the town square – drunken smokers mock Colin

Neds and young farmers determined to gull him

But Colin won't take no shite – Kung Fu Colin shocks them

A head knock – a fist chop – a kick-boxing Jackie Chan

Till alone and bloody – bold Colin walks darkly

Through Kelso suburbs to Asda car park

Light as breath he walks – a beer-bellied ninja.

Cat-eyed Colin the searcher – the assassin from Perth

Alert as an atom to the slightest shiver of universe.

Wolf Colin sniffs the air – ooo ooo ooo oooooow.

ONE COLIN SYME
THERE'S ONLY ONE COLIN SYME
ONE COLIN SY – IME
THERE'S ONLY ONE COLIN SY – IME.

Silence.

Then *crack* – the sky splits open. Right there beside him.

A wild cut of light tears the darkness apart.

What the fuck! – Colin shits himself.

Bean-tiny testicles – shrink in his abdomen.

But then a voice calls to him – a hand in the darkness:

HELP! HELP! I NEED A HAND! IS ANYBODY THERE!

The voice is Prudencia's – Colin Syme's balls descend
again.

Colin turns and he sees fair Prudencia's hand.

'Over here Pru!' – bold Colin calls –

'Pru hold on – grab on to me!'

Syme-heart, The Big Syme – The Sensational Colin Syme
Band.

Cock Colin – all swaggering – certain of victory.

'I am the Tartan Army at Wembley.'

ONE COLIN SYME
THERE'S ONLY ONE COLIN SYME
ONE COLIN SY – IME
THERE'S ONLY ONE COLIN SY – IME.

SIXTEEN

The midnight bells ring.

Dong.

Prudencia Hold on to me, Colin. I know this ballad. In this one the Devil changes me into all sorts of horrible things. No matter what happens you must hold on. Don't let go!

Colin Got you, Pru!
  Jesus Christ – you're an eel!

Prudencia I'm not an eel, Colin, I'm still Prudencia. The Devil who's got me's putting thoughts in your head.

Devil Let her go, mortal! – This fish is mine now.

Prudencia turned fish now – mucus and teeth now
Eel breath and tongue now – slippery and stink.

Devil Let her go, mortal!

But Colin held on.

  Dong.

Devil How about fire then? How'd you like that, mortal?

Colin Ayaaaah, ya bastard.

Prudencia Hold on, Colin – don't let go.

Colin Jings crivvens. It's burnie!

Prudencia ablaze now,
Her body a bonfire – his skin burned to toast.

Prudencia It's not real fire, Colin, its all imaginary –

Devil Let her go, mortal!

But Colin held on.

Dong.

Devil If you defy me – mortal – you'll pay the price –
let's see if you can hold on to a girl made of ice.

Colin Oh, for fuck's sake.

Prudencia It's not real, Colin.

Colin It feels fucking real.

The temperature fell to minus forty now
The wind like a knife from the Arctic blew now
Prudencia gripped his frozen hand.

Prudencia Colin, focus – it's me, Colin – it's all in the
mind, Colin.

Devil Let her go, mortal!

But Colin held on.

Dong.

Fifth bell scorpions.

Dong.

Next bell a rockfall.

Five more mutations Prudencia went through.

Each time Colin held on – Prudencia safe.

Till finally – eleven struck – here was the last bell.

Prudencia This is it, Colin, hold on, just one change
more.

Colin Do your worst, Devil – change her into what you
like. My love is chaste and as pure as a knight.

Devil Prudencia, please.

Prudencia I'm sorry.

Devil No.

> *Dong.*
>> *Flash.*

And with that final midnight tolling –
Like a polling station at the end of polling –
Time's wound closed up – scabbed over – sealed.
The Devil drew back to Hell in shame concealed.
Poor Prudencia was scratched, dishevelled,
Clothes and skin torn where the Devil'd
Held her, but psychologically she was OK – she'd
     made it.
'There's only one Colin Syme,' she said, kissed him,
     then faded
Fell back in the snow unconsciously
And Colin for a second stood before – exhausted – so
     did he.

ONE COLIN SYME
THERE'S ONLY ONE COLIN SYME
ONE COLIN SY – IME
THERE'S ONLY ONE COLIN SY – IME.

SEVENTEEN

Prudencia and Colin awaken in the snow.
  Both are dishevelled.

[*Dialogue separated with a / indicates it is spoken
simultaneously by both Colin and Prudencia.*]

— Colin?

Prudencia?

— Hello. / Hello.

What are you? / What are you?

— I don't know. / I don't know.

Pause.

— Colin.

Yes.

— What year is it?

2010.

. . .

Why?

— I just – I'd forgotten.

. . .

Are you sure?

Certain.

— That's all right then.

Pause. Embarrassed at their own dishevelment and nakedness.

— Goodness. / Goodness.

Pause.

— Where are we? / Where are we?

— It's dark.

I think it's Asda car park.

Pause.

— What happened? / What happened?

I don't remember. / I don't remember.

I was tremendously drunk.

— Me too.

Tremendously – tremendously drunk.

— I was looking for the B and B.

I was looking for you.

— I got lost.

Me too.

— I must have just lain down in the snow.

Same here.

— Embarrassing. / Embarrassing.

What time is it?

Just past half past two.

— You must be cold. / You must be cold.

— Very. / Very.

Maybe we should go back to the old
Pub or . . . do you want to go to the B and B?

— No.

Nor me.
. . .
One of the guys at the pub gave me the impression that
After midnight they switch off the karaoke and have a
session – a proper session.

— Sounds good.

Would you like to go?

— I would.
Colin.

Yes.

— Did we . . . ?

  Beat.

88

I don't know. / I don't know.

Gosh. / Gosh.

Bish bash bosh. / Bish bash bosh.

EIGHTEEN

Back in the pub.

The pub was heaving – far from bereft it
Was heaving as if they'd never left it.
Professor Macintosh led the ceilidh
Playing comic songs on the banjolele
Siolaigh sang an Irish Gaelic song
Step-dancing naked but for a green thong
Which both helped her interpret the ancient verse
And demonstrated the quality of her Erse.
Colin and Pru melted easily into the crowd
Hot and smoky and fleshy and loud
And here were the harpies lying – placid
On downers now – or was it acid?
And in the corner, flaccid – spent –
Geoff – and the bald men. Prudencia went
To join them because she wanted to know
'Who was the woman I saw singing in the snow,
The strange woman who sang "Blackwaterside"?'
Oh her – that sounds like the lassie that died –
'Died?' – Last winter just as the year was turning
She was drunk on the sofa – left a fag burning
Awful really – alkie – they say she hit the drink
After an affair with – Nick up at Goodman's Hill I think,
Aye, that's right – there was rumours of a romance,
The whole house went up – poor woman had no chance
Neither did her kids. Shame – she was a lovely singer.
'What happened to Nick?' – Don't know – there's
      rumours he's a swinger.

Stunned Prudencia was beginning to feel
That none of what happened to her had been real.
Maybe it had all been an hypothermic dream
Caused by anxiety and extreme
Cold – she remembered Hell, the Devil's place
And she couldn't even recall his face.

Prudencia! Old girl.

— Professor Macintosh?

It's your turn for a turn –

— A turn – Gosh . . . must I?

Indeed you must – we've all given ours,
Get up here now and let's hear yours.

The revelry was still in full swing.
The whole pub chanted:

Sing! Sing! Sing!

Prudencia gets up to sing.

— I really don't . . . I . . . I'm not sure . . .

Prudencia stood – vulnerable and raw.
She looked out at the crowd and then she saw
Outside – at the window, standing there,
It was him – standing all alone in the square.
The Devil – and to her surprise
He seemed to have tears in his eyes.
And Prudencia – in that moment – knew
To find your song – you first find who to sing it to.
And hers was him – her companion of two millennia.

What song are you going to sing, Prudencia?

— This is . . . a little something for an old friend.

Said Prudencia slyly.

'Not so much Devil's Ceilidh as the Devil's Kylie.'

NINETEEN

Prudencia steps up to the microphone and sings. The song she sings is full of yearning and loss, the song she sings is a love song . . . Ideally the song she sings is Kylie Minogue's 'I Can't Get You Out of My Head'.

As Prudencia sings, the Devil appears in the window of the bar, looking in.

He reaches out to the glass.

As Prudencia's song gathers force smoke comes from her mouth, her eyes turn read, blood drips from the end of her fingers.

Prudencia sings the story to its end.

UNIVERSITY OF WINCHESTER LIBRARY